Cougar Kittens

written by VICTORIA MILES
illustrated by LORNA KEARNEY

ORCA BOOK PUBLISHERS

One early summer morning a hungry mother cougar rises from her bed beneath a fallen Hemlock tree. She slips quietly into the dim light, leaving behind three sleeping kittens.

A sunbeam reaches down through the forest and the kittens open their eyes. The two brother kittens and their sister stretch and chirp, calling for their mother. But she is too far away now to hear their small voices.

From their hiding place, Sister watches
a dragonfly balancing upon a shrub
nearby. The dragonfly's wings shimmer
in the sunshine. The brothers do not
notice it. They are too busy chasing
each other's tails.

Sister crouches down, crawls forward and pounces . . . but the dragonfly is too quick for the young kitten. It hovers safely out of her reach before flying out of sight.

Now the trembling bush is the game. All three kittens attack its branches, but the bush is not much of a playmate — it does not fight back. After a while the kittens tire of this battle. Instead they roll, leap and tumble together over the forest floor.

One brother kitten is hungry. He trots over to the covering of dirt and twigs that his mother scraped over a deer. There is nothing left of it to eat.

A strong smell in the air startles all three kittens at once. They are not alone anymore. Frightened, their sharp claws spring from their front paws as they bolt up into the trees. Balancing on branches, the kittens stare down to the ground far below.

A wolf enters the thicket, sniffing about. There is no food for him here either and so he goes away.

Late in the afternoon, mother cougar returns. *Ma-ow! Ma-ow! Ma-ow!* she calls sharply to her young as she nears the thicket. Hearing her call, the tired kittens answer her with high, bird-like chirps. They scramble down from the trees and scamper over to her. She purrs and licks them with her rough tongue.

Calling for her family to follow, mother cougar begins the long journey to the shady hollow where she has hidden another deer.

As the kittens grow, their world becomes
wider. They roam with Mother through more
and more of her range.

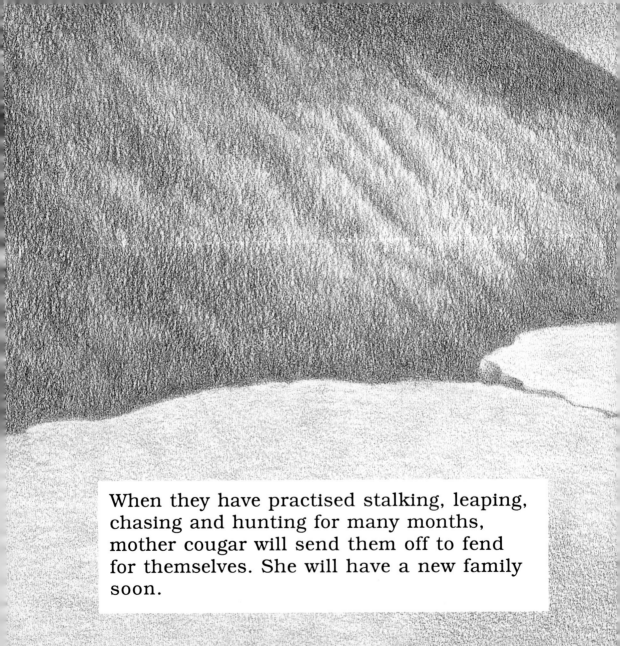

When they have practised stalking, leaping, chasing and hunting for many months, mother cougar will send them off to fend for themselves. She will have a new family soon.

At one time, the cougar (*Felis concolor*) had the greatest range of any land mammal in the western world. Today, in the eastern United States, cougars have vanished from all but pockets of their former territory. This disappearance was largely caused by vigorous control programs, human settlement and conversion of cougar country into agricultural land. Healthy cougar populations continue to exist in western North America where prey and habitat is still sufficient to support them.

The author and illustrator gratefully acknowledge the contributions of cougar biologists Dr. Maurice Hornocker, Knut Atkinson, Martin Jalkotzy and Ian Ross to this book. In addition, we thank Cris Guppy, M.Sc. and conservationist Sherry Pettigrew for their advice, and Ted Chappell for guiding us to view a cougar in the wild.

For understanding
V.M.
Especially for Katy
L.K.

Text copyright © 1995 Victoria Miles
Illustration copyright © 1995 Lorna Kearney

Publication assistance provided by The Canada Council.
All rights reserved.

Orca Book Publishers
PO Box 5626, Station B
Victoria, BC Canada
V8R 6S4

Orca Book Publishers
PO Box 468
Custer, WA   USA
98240-0468

10 9 8 7 6 5 4 3 2 1

Canadian Cataloguing in Publication Data
Miles, Victoria, 1966 —
    Cougar kittens

    ISBN 1-55143-026-6
    1. Pumas — Juvenile literature. I.
Kearney, Lorna, 1943– II. Title.
QL737.C23M54 1995   j599.74′428   C95–910215

Design by Christine Toller
Printed and bound in Hong Kong